Reverse Psychology

Alexa Murphy

Alexa Murphy

Copyright Page

Copyright Holder: © 2024, Andrea Jimenez
Year: 2024
Author: © 2024, Alexa Murph

Legal and Copyright Information

Index

Introduction to Reverse Psychology

Reverse psychology is a persuasion technique that has been present in our lives much more than we imagine. We have all, at some point, been victims or have used this technique, without even realizing it. But what exactly is reverse psychology? In simple terms, it is the art of making someone do what we want, but in a subtle and almost contrary way. Instead of asking or insisting on something directly, we suggest the opposite, triggering in the person a desire to do exactly the opposite of what has been suggested.

Imagine you tell a child not to play with a particular toy. If the child wasn't interested in that toy before, chances are that after your ban, they'll suddenly want it badly. This impulse to do the opposite of what they're told is what makes reverse psychology work so well. And not just on children. Adults fall into these kinds of psychological traps too, because it's part of how our minds work.

Our mind tends to react in the opposite way when we feel that our freedom of choice is being threatened. This is what is known as psychological resistance. When someone tells us what to do or what not to do, we feel, often without being aware of it, an impulse to demonstrate our autonomy, to make our own decisions, even if these decisions go against what was initially suggested to us. Reverse psychology takes advantage of this natural mechanism.

The fascinating thing is that this type of manipulation can be used in very simple ways or in more complex contexts, from parenting to work relationships, and even in advertising. Often, the messages we receive are designed to arouse this type of resistance in us. Think of an advertisement that says something like, "Only for the brave." This type of phrase is designed to make people feel that if they don't buy that product or take that action, then they are not brave enough, and they will naturally want to prove otherwise.

Reverse psychology is a powerful tool because it taps into human nature at its most basic: the desire to be independent and to make decisions for ourselves.

However, the interesting thing is that, many times, people who fall under its influence don't realize that they have been guided into an action they weren't initially planning to take. And this is what makes this technique so effective, as it doesn't feel like an imposition, but rather like a decision of their own.

In everyday life, reverse psychology can be seen in many everyday examples. For example, a boss who wants his employees to be more responsible might say, "This project is probably too difficult for you." This statement might spark in employees a desire to prove that they can handle it, leading to increased effort from the team. Similarly, in personal relationships, a partner might say something like, "I don't think you'll be able to remember our anniversary." This statement might cause the other person, in an attempt to contradict that statement, to make an effort to remember the date and do something special.

But why does reverse psychology work so well? The answer lies in how our minds work.

When we feel that our freedom is threatened, we tend to rebel. If someone tells us "you can't do this," we immediately feel the need to prove that we can indeed do it. This drive to prove our independence and competence is deeply human. What's more, reverse psychology plays on our expectations and desires for challenge. When we are presented with a limit or restriction, our nature drives us to break it, to prove that we can do the opposite.

Throughout history, reverse psychology has been used in different contexts, from education to politics and advertising. Leaders have known how to use it to influence the decisions of the masses, parents have used it to guide the behavior of their children, and advertisers have managed to sell products by playing on the emotions of their consumers. The most interesting thing is that, although it seems like a complex technique, it is actually very simple to apply. You just have to understand how people react when a limit or expectation is placed on them, and use that reaction to your advantage.

In short, reverse psychology is a powerful technique that relies on our natural tendency to resist when we feel our decisions are being controlled. It works by provoking a contrary reaction in people, causing them to make the decision we want, even though it may seem like they are acting of their own free will. It is a tool that, when used wisely, can be very effective, but it can also be dangerous if abused.

The Origin of Reverse Psychology

The origin of reverse psychology can be traced back to fundamental concepts within psychology and human behavior, although the technique itself was not formally studied until the 20th century. However, long before psychologists began to examine it, reverse psychology was already present in our everyday interactions. The tendency of people to resist direct orders or to act contrary to what they are told has been a human characteristic throughout history, and various cultures and traditions have recognized it in different ways.

One of the first to formally study this phenomenon was social psychologist Jack Brehm, who in the 1960s developed the theory of "psychological reactance." This theory holds that when individuals feel that their freedom is being limited, they experience an emotional reaction that drives them to restore that freedom. Put another way, when we feel that someone is trying to control us or impose a decision, our instinct leads us to want to do the opposite, simply to prove that we are in control of our own decisions. This idea of reactance is key to understanding how and why reverse psychology works.

The concept of psychological reactance may seem new, but if we stop to think about it, it was already present long before Brehm described it. For example, in ancient philosophy and in the teachings of various religions, we find references to human resistance to authority or imposed norms. Greek philosophers, such as Socrates and Plato, already spoke of the contradictory nature of human beings and how we often do the opposite of what is expected of us. In certain religious texts, there are also stories in which the prohibition of doing something leads people, in their desire to challenge the norm, to disobey, as in the famous story of Adam and Eve in the Garden of Eden.

Reverse psychology is not simply a modern invention. Stories, myths, and tales from different cultures show us how people have always had a tendency to rebel against prohibitions or mandates. In the Middle Ages, for example, rulers and religious leaders often used severe restrictions to control the masses, but these restrictions also sometimes led to the opposite effect. Banning the consumption of certain books or ideas, for example, made those same ideas even more attractive to those who felt deprived of access to them. This "I want what I can't have" reaction is a clear example of how reverse psychology can be at play even when it is not intentionally planned.

Another relevant case in history where we see the implicit use of reverse psychology is in military strategies. Throughout the centuries, military leaders have employed psychological tactics to demoralize their enemies or incite them to act impulsively. The idea of "challenging" the enemy, making them feel that they are not capable of facing a challenge, often pushes them to make reckless decisions, exactly what the leader wants. Although it was not called "reverse psychology" in those times, the underlying principles were the same.

Over time, reverse psychology became a more formal subject of study within psychology. In the 20th century, with the rise of behavioral psychology and social psychology, studies began to be conducted to better understand how people respond to commands and how psychological resistance plays a key role in our decisions. In addition to Jack Brehm, other researchers such as Leon Festinger, with his theory of cognitive dissonance, also influenced the understanding of people's contradictory behavior in the face of societal expectations. Cognitive dissonance describes how people tend to experience discomfort when their beliefs or actions are not aligned, which can lead them to justify their behaviors even if they go against what they rationally know is best for them.

As research progressed, psychologists began to notice that reverse psychology applied not only to individuals, but also to groups. Group dynamics, such as those seen in social or work contexts, showed that people as a whole can also resist direct commands or suggestions, reacting in the opposite way out of a simple desire to maintain their autonomy. Thus, reverse psychology began to be used in a more structured way in areas such as advertising, marketing, and education.

In advertising, for example, messages that appear to "discourage" consumers from buying certain products actually encourage them to do so. Phrases like "This product is only for the daring" or "Not everyone can handle it" create a sense of challenge that makes people want to prove they can. Advertisers have realized that by subtly suggesting that a consumer is not capable of doing something, they are awakened in a desire to prove otherwise.

Reverse psychology has also found a place in parenting and education. Although not always intentionally, many parents and teachers have used this technique to guide children's behavior. For example, by saying, "I don't think you'll be able to finish your homework before dinner," a child may feel compelled to prove that he or she is capable by completing the task quickly. Although this strategy can be effective, its use must be careful, as overuse of reverse psychology can lead to children becoming rebellious or distrustful of adults' intentions.

Over time, reverse psychology has come to be recognized not only as a useful tactic, but as a reflection of our human nature. We all have an inherent desire to demonstrate our independence and our ability to make decisions for ourselves. Reverse psychology taps into this desire in subtle ways, making people feel like they are making decisions on their own, when in reality they are being influenced in a strategic way.

In short, although the term "reverse psychology" may sound modern, its essence has been present in human behavior since ancient times. The evolution of its study, from ancient philosophical ideas to modern psychological studies, shows us that this technique is deeply rooted in how we think and act. And although it may seem like a simple manipulation strategy, it actually reflects a fundamental part of our psychology: the desire to be free in our decisions and to resist when we feel that freedom is in danger.

How Reverse Psychology Works in the Brain

To understand how reverse psychology works in the brain, we first need to think about how our minds react when we feel like we are being controlled or manipulated. The human brain has a fascinating ability to identify and resist situations where our freedom of choice is threatened. This natural resistance is the key behind how reverse psychology works. What happens is that when someone gives us an order or tells us to do something in a direct way, our brain can interpret this as an invasion of our autonomy, which triggers an emotional response known as psychological reactance.

Psychological reactance is a phenomenon that occurs in our brain when we perceive that our freedom is being limited. It is an automatic response that we often don't even notice, but that drives us to want to do exactly the opposite of what we have been asked to do. This mechanism is designed to protect our sense of freedom, something that is fundamental to our emotional well-being. When someone tells us "don't do this," our brain activates an internal alert that pushes us to restore that freedom of action that we think we are losing. So, when we feel that someone is trying to control us, we resist, and reverse psychology takes advantage of this natural impulse.

The brain has several regions involved in this process. One of the most important is the prefrontal cortex, which is related to decision-making and controlling our impulses. This part of the brain helps us assess situations and decide what is the best course of action to take. However, when it senses that a decision is being imposed externally, it can trigger a feeling of rejection, leading us to do exactly the opposite of what is expected of us. In essence, the brain interprets the situation as a kind of challenge, and the desire to restore our autonomy becomes a priority.

Another area involved is the limbic system, the part of the brain responsible for our emotions. Psychological reactance is largely an emotional reaction, and the limbic system plays a key role in it. When someone tells us what to do or what not to do, the limbic system generates an emotional response that can range from frustration to irritation. This emotional response reinforces the desire to go against what we have been told, as we feel emotionally uncomfortable with the idea of losing control over our decisions.

But the brain doesn't stop there. The nucleus accumbens, a region related to reward and pleasure, also comes into play. When we decide to act against what we've been told, this part of the brain rewards us with a feeling of satisfaction. It's as if the brain rewards us for defying an imposition, making us feel good about regaining our freedom. This internal reward reinforces the contrary behavior, making us more likely to act against what we've been told on future occasions.

Reverse psychology, then, works because it exploits this delicate balance between external control and the internal need for autonomy. By suggesting the opposite of what we want someone to do, we trigger in their brain the feeling that they are being offered a choice, allowing them to feel in control of the situation. For example, if you tell someone that they probably can't complete a task because it's too difficult, their brain may interpret this as a challenge. The prefrontal cortex assesses the situation and the person feels the urge to prove otherwise, restoring their freedom of action while at the same time gaining a sense of accomplishment and satisfaction when they succeed.

This type of brain functioning may also explain why reverse psychology is so effective in situations where a person feels that their pride or competence is at stake. By making a suggestion that indirectly challenges someone's capabilities, you stimulate their need to prove that they can do it. Here, it's not just the desire for freedom that's at play, but also the desire for recognition and self-affirmation. The brain hates the idea of feeling limited or underestimated, so it often reacts by doing exactly the opposite of what has been suggested.

An interesting aspect is that reverse psychology doesn't only work when another person challenges us; we can also use it on ourselves. This happens when we give ourselves mental commands, for example, when we try to force ourselves to do something that we know we should do, but don't want to do. If we tell ourselves "you can't do it," the brain can activate the same reactance mechanism, leading us to perform the task just to prove that we are capable. This type of self-challenge can be useful in contexts of personal motivation, where reverse psychology can be applied intentionally to self-stimulate.

It is important to note that reverse psychology does not always work the same way for everyone. Some studies suggest that people with a strong need for autonomy or those who have a more rebellious personality tend to be more susceptible to this type of manipulation. Their brain is more predisposed to resist direct orders, which makes them more likely to act against what they are told. On the other hand, people who are more conformist or who do not feel the same need to defend their freedom may be less sensitive to reverse psychology, since their brain does not react as strongly to impositions.

In short, reverse psychology works in the brain because it taps into our innate desire to be independent and make our own decisions. When we feel like our freedom is at risk, the brain activates a series of responses that drive us to regain that sense of control, even if it means doing the opposite of what we've been told. Psychological reactance, emotional response, and reward for challenging ourselves are the key mechanisms that make reverse psychology so effective. And while it may seem like a simple trick, it's actually a strategy deeply rooted in the way our brains handle decisions and autonomy.

Reverse Psychology in Everyday Life

Reverse psychology is a powerful tool that we often use without even realizing it. It is present in many daily interactions, whether in our relationships with friends, family, coworkers, or even strangers. It is a technique that, by making a suggestion contrary to what we really want, causes the other person to do exactly what we wanted all along. Although it sounds like a complicated trick, the reality is that we do it so naturally that it almost goes unnoticed. The reason it works so well is because it appeals to our basic need to feel in control of our decisions, something we all value.

One of the most common examples of reverse psychology occurs in parenting. Parents often use it, often unintentionally, to guide their children's behavior. For example, if a child refuses to pick up his or her toys, instead of telling the child to do so directly, a parent might say, "Don't worry, I'm sure you're too young to pick up all those toys by yourself." Upon hearing this, the child may feel challenged and decide that he or she can actually do it, and will do it just to prove otherwise. This is a simple, yet very effective example of how reverse psychology can work in everyday situations, making the person act according to our wishes without feeling pressured.

Another context where we often see reverse psychology is in romantic relationships. Sometimes, when we want our partner to do something, but we don't want to seem bossy or pushy, we use reverse psychology to get them to take the initiative. For example, if someone wants their partner to organize an outing, instead of directly saying, "I want to make plans for this weekend," they might say, "I don't think there's anything interesting to do this weekend." Hearing this might motivate the other person to prove that there are many interesting things to do and end up organizing a special outing or plan. It's a subtle way to guide a situation without creating confrontation or resistance.

Reverse psychology is also used in advertising and marketing, although we often don't notice it. Brands and advertisers have learned to leverage this principle to influence consumers. Think of advertising campaigns that use phrases like "Not everyone can handle this product" or "Only the bravest will dare to try it." These types of messages are designed to make you feel like if you don't buy the product, you're missing out on something unique or that you lack courage. The human brain responds to these types of challenges because we don't like to feel limited or incompetent, so we're tempted to do the opposite of what is indirectly suggested to us, buying the product just to prove that we can handle it or that we're brave enough.

In the workplace, reverse psychology can also be very useful. Imagine a boss wants his team to work faster or complete a particularly difficult task. Instead of putting pressure on them directly or imposing strict deadlines, he might say, "I understand that this may be too complicated, maybe we need to lower expectations." Hearing this, the team might feel motivated to prove that they can indeed handle the task and, in the end, deliver better work than if they had been forced directly. People at work often respond better when they feel like they are making decisions on their own and not because something has been imposed on them in an authoritarian manner.

Friendships are also a place where reverse psychology can naturally arise. For example, if a friend is not interested in attending a meeting or event, instead of directly insisting that they go, you might say something like, "Don't worry, it's probably not your type of event, you probably wouldn't have fun." This seemingly easy-out statement may actually spark a desire to prove that they might enjoy it or are more open-minded than they are given to believe, and they may ultimately decide to attend just to prove that perception wrong. It's a common social tactic, used in informal situations to manage others' expectations and desires without appearing controlling.

In our daily lives, we also find ourselves using reverse psychology on ourselves. Sometimes, when we don't feel like doing something important, like cleaning the house or finishing a pending task, our brains may respond better to a small internal challenge.

If we tell ourselves, "You probably won't be able to finish this today," we might activate an impulse to prove otherwise and do it just to feel good about ourselves. Even though we may not know it, we are using reverse psychology to motivate ourselves, because our brains respond well to challenges when we believe we have something to prove, even to ourselves.

One area where reverse psychology is also very effective is in education. Teachers and educators, often in subtle ways, use it to motivate students. If a teacher notices that a student is not paying attention or is not interested in participating in an activity, instead of urging the student to do so, they might say something like, "I'm not sure you're ready for this kind of challenge." This small affirmation can make the student, wanting to prove that they are ready, feel more committed to participating and getting involved in the activity. This technique can be particularly helpful with children and adolescents, who often feel driven to prove that they can do more than others expect of them.

In short, reverse psychology is a tool that we use naturally in our daily lives, without needing to be experts in psychology. Whether it is to motivate a child to do something they don't want to do, to influence a partner to make a decision, to convince a friend to participate in a plan or even to motivate ourselves to complete a task, reverse psychology is present in many situations. It works because it takes advantage of our tendency to resist impositions and to want to demonstrate our autonomy. When we feel that we are in control and that our decisions are our own, we are more willing to act, even if that means doing exactly the opposite of what was initially suggested to us. It is a subtle, but very effective technique, and, when used appropriately, it can facilitate our daily interactions and help us achieve our goals without generating conflict or resistance.

Alexa Murphy

The Key to Rejection

Rejection is an inevitable part of life, and although we often see it as something negative, it is fundamental to understanding why reverse psychology works so well. The key to rejection is how we react when we feel that someone is imposing something on us, even if what they are suggesting is something that could actually benefit us. When we perceive that our freedom of choice is being threatened, a kind of automatic impulse arises that leads us to reject that imposition. This reaction may seem illogical, but it makes a lot of sense when we understand how the human mind works.

Rejection, in this context, is a natural response to anything that seems to limit our autonomy. As humans, we place a high value on our ability to make our own decisions. From a young age, we learn to want to feel independent, to make our own choices, and to show that we can do things for ourselves. This desire for independence grows stronger over time, and when someone tells us what to do or how to act, it's as if our brains put up a defensive barrier. We feel like we need to protect our ability to decide, and often the best way to do that, in our minds, is to reject what we're told.

Imagine, for example, that someone tells you, "You should exercise every day." Even though deep down you know that it's good advice, a part of you might feel that this suggestion is limiting your freedom. You might even feel a little internal resistance, as if the mere fact that someone is telling you what to do is pushing you to do the opposite. This is rejection in action. It's not that you don't understand the benefits of exercise, but that you feel that it wasn't your initial choice, and that makes you resist. This is where reverse psychology can come into play, taking advantage of that tendency to reject.

What really triggers rejection is the desire to feel like our choices are our own. When something feels like an imposition, we feel like we're not making free choices, and that can create discomfort that leads to rejection. Reverse psychology takes advantage of this natural reaction. Instead of telling yourself,

"You should exercise," you might suggest something like, "You probably won't have time to exercise today; you're probably too busy." This seemingly pressure-relieving phrase can actually cause your brain to react differently. Instead of feeling rejected, you might feel motivated to prove otherwise, saying to yourself, "I do have time, and I will."

This tendency to reject what is imposed on us is deeply rooted in our nature. As children, when we begin to discover the world for ourselves, we are faced with situations where we are told what to do or what not to do. Parents, with the best of intentions, often tell us things like "don't touch that" or "don't do that," which generates curiosity and an almost automatic impulse to do just the opposite. This is not just childish rebellion, it is a reflection of the human mind seeking its own space for decision-making. As we grow up, this tendency does not disappear, it simply becomes more subtle.

Rejection isn't always a conscious thing. Sometimes, we don't even realize that we're rejecting an idea or suggestion simply because we feel like it's being forced on us. This can happen at work, when a boss tells us how we should do something, or in our relationships, when someone gives us unsolicited advice. The moment we feel like we have no control over the situation, our mind starts looking for ways to regain that control, and one of the simplest ways to do that is by rejecting the suggestion or doing the opposite of what we've been told.

The interesting thing is that rejection isn't just about going against others, it also happens when we give ourselves certain mental orders. For example, if you tell yourself "I have to stop eating so many sweets," you may notice that, instead of reducing your consumption, you feel more tempted to eat even more. This is because, even when the "order" comes from yourself, the brain can interpret it as a restriction and react in the same way, seeking to regain that feeling of freedom by rejecting the idea. This phenomenon is what often makes diets or personal resolutions so difficult to maintain.

Rejection, then, is not just a negative response, but a natural defense that the brain uses to protect what it perceives as its freedom. But what makes reverse psychology so effective is that it leverages this same mechanism to direct behavior in the direction we want. By suggesting the opposite of what we actually desire, we are tricking the mind a little into feeling like it is in control, and instead of rejecting what is proposed, it chooses to do it on its own. The trick is knowing how to present the situation in a way that doesn't feel like an imposition.

Another fascinating aspect of the rejection cue is how it works differently in different people. Some individuals have a greater tendency to reject any kind of authority or control, while others may be more conformist or more likely to accept suggestions without as much conflict. However, even in those who are more accommodating, reverse psychology can have an impact, because we all have a basic desire for autonomy, even if we don't express it in the same way.

It's important to understand that rejection isn't always negative. In fact, it can be a useful tool in everyday life. It helps us stay true to what we want and stand by our choices. However, when we understand how this mechanism works, we can also learn to manage it more effectively, both in ourselves and in our interactions with others. The key is to recognize when we're experiencing that natural rejection reaction and think of ways to reframe our actions or words to avoid triggering it.

Reverse psychology, in short, works because it understands the power of rejection and uses it to its advantage. Instead of fighting that natural tendency to resist when we feel like we're losing control, it allows us to create a scenario where the other person feels like they're making their own decisions, even if those decisions coincide with what we wanted all along. This is the heart of the technique: harnessing the impulse of rejection to guide behavior without confrontation, without imposition, and without the person feeling pressured or manipulated. It's a subtle, but powerful way to influence others while respecting their need for autonomy.

Applications in Parenting

Parenting is one of the contexts where reverse psychology is most frequently used, even though many parents may not realize they are using it. Raising a child is no easy task. Children, from a very young age, begin to develop their own sense of independence, and this can often conflict with parental instructions or expectations. When a child feels that they are being forced to do something they do not want to do or that they are being prevented from doing something they want to do, they often respond with resistance. This is where reverse psychology comes in as a subtle and effective tool to guide behavior without directly imposing it.

One of the most common examples of reverse psychology in parenting is mealtime. Imagine a child who doesn't want to eat his vegetables. The direct approach, such as "Eat your vegetables, they're good for you," often leads to more resistance. The child may feel like he's being coerced and will refuse to eat them, not necessarily because he doesn't like them, but because he wants to demonstrate his control over the situation.

Instead of insisting, a parent might say something like, "You probably don't like these vegetables, I don't think you can eat them all." Upon hearing this, the child, sensing the challenge, might decide to eat them, simply to prove that he's capable. This little trick of reverse psychology plays on the child's desire to make his own decisions, leading him to do what the parent wants without feeling like he's lost control.

Another common example is toy pick-up time. Many children resist tidying up tasks, especially if they are deep in play and don't want the fun time to end. Instead of directly telling a child to pick up his or her toys, a parent can employ reverse psychology by saying something like, "Don't worry, I know picking up all those toys is too hard for you, maybe we should do it another day." The child, wanting to prove that he or she is capable of doing it, might immediately start picking up the toys, with the idea that he or she is taking control of the situation. What seemed like initial resistance turns into cooperation, all because the child was given the feeling that the decision was his or hers.

These types of techniques are also useful in situations where children are learning to dress themselves or complete small everyday tasks. If a parent tells their child, "I doubt you can dress yourself, it must be too complicated," the child will likely want to prove that they can do it and try harder. The key here is not to make the suggestion sound like a taunt, but rather a neutral comment that subtly challenges the child's abilities. The goal is not to make the child feel bad, but to motivate them to prove that they are more capable than they think.

Reverse psychology can also be helpful in situations where parents want their children to make responsible choices. For example, if a child doesn't want to do his or her homework, rather than forcing him or her to do it, a parent might say, "Well, maybe you don't have time to do your homework today, or maybe you'd rather take a break and not finish it." The child, feeling like he or she is being given the option of not doing the homework, might reconsider and decide to do it to avoid the natural consequences of not doing it. The feeling of freedom, even if it is an illusion, allows him or her to make a choice that benefits him or her, and avoids the direct confrontation that often creates conflict.

The interesting thing about reverse psychology in parenting is that it not only helps to resolve specific situations, but it also strengthens the relationship between parents and children. When children feel that everything is not being imposed on them directly, they are more likely to cooperate voluntarily. This approach respects their need for autonomy and allows them to feel that they are making decisions for themselves, which is crucial for their emotional development. By using reverse psychology, parents are not forcing their children to act in a particular way, but are gently guiding them towards the desired behavior.

Another area where reverse psychology can be very effective is in discipline. Sometimes children behave in defiant ways simply because they are seeking attention or want to test the limits of what they can do. Instead of reacting with anger or outright punishment, a parent might apply reverse psychology by saying something like, "I don't think you're interested in behaving today, you'd probably rather keep doing whatever you want." This statement, which is neither aggressive nor punitive, can lead the child to reconsider his or her behavior and act more appropriately, just to prove that he or she can behave well. Instead of feeling like they are being punished or controlled, children respond to these types of suggestions with a more positive attitude change.

It is important to note that reverse psychology should not be used as constant or excessive manipulation. Children are very intelligent and if they sense that they are always being tricked, they may lose trust in their parents or become frustrated. The key is to use this technique in a balanced way, as one more tool in the toolbox for parenting, not as the only method. Honesty and open communication are just as important, but reverse psychology can be a fun and creative way to deal with certain everyday challenges.

One key thing to consider is that reverse psychology works best when used in moments where the child is already showing resistance or when the direct approach has failed. It doesn't need to be applied in every situation, as sometimes children respond well to clear, direct communication. However, in those moments where nothing seems to be working, turning to reverse psychology can be a way to defuse tension and achieve cooperation without the child feeling like he or she is losing his or her freedom of choice.

In more complex situations, such as helping children develop good habits, reverse psychology can be a useful tool in the long run. If a child doesn't want to brush his or her teeth before bed, a parent might say, "I don't think it's that important to brush your teeth every night, maybe you don't need to do it today." Although this statement goes against what is actually desired, the child's defiant nature may lead him or her to do just the opposite, seeking to assert his or her independence. As the child begins to make this task a habit, the use of reverse psychology can be reduced, as cooperation and desired behavior are more established.

Ultimately, parenting is a challenging process, and every child is different. What works for one may not work for another, but reverse psychology offers a versatile tool that can be adapted to many situations. Children, like adults, value their autonomy, and when they feel they have control over their decisions, they are more likely to willingly cooperate. Reverse psychology, used carefully and respectfully, can make parenting a little more bearable and daily interactions with children more harmonious.

In short, reverse psychology in parenting is a subtle way to influence children's behavior without creating conflict or forcing things. By presenting a suggestion in a way that doesn't feel like an imposition, parents can guide their children toward positive behaviors, while strengthening their sense of independence. It's an effective technique, but it should be used sparingly and always with the goal of helping the child grow in a healthy and autonomous way.

Reverse Psychology in Couple Relationships

Reverse psychology in romantic relationships may seem like a sensitive topic, but it is a technique that can be used effectively to improve communication and strengthen the connection between two people. Romantic relationships are often filled with emotions, expectations, and sometimes misunderstandings. Often, when a partner feels pressured or pushed into doing something, the natural reaction is to resist or reject the idea, even if deep down they agree. Reverse psychology, when used tactfully and respectfully, can help smooth out these situations and encourage cooperation without the other person feeling like they are being manipulated or controlled.

In the context of a relationship, reverse psychology is not intended to manipulate or deceive the other person, but is used to overcome resistance that arises when someone feels they are losing their freedom or decision-making power. For example, in many cases, one partner may want the other to participate more in household chores, but if they express this too directly, such as by saying "you need to do more around the house," this can lead to a negative reaction. The other person may feel that they are being criticized or not valued enough, which can lead to an argument or a lack of cooperation.

This is where reverse psychology can come in handy. Instead of directly demanding that your partner do more around the house, you could say something like, "I know you're really busy, you probably don't have time to help with chores today." This approach, which seems to release the other person from responsibility, can make them feel motivated to prove otherwise and end up helping out, not because you asked them to, but because they feel it was their decision. Instead of feeling like they're giving in to a demand, they feel empowered to act on their own.

Another example could be related to making important decisions, such as choosing a vacation spot or a weekend plan. In many relationships, a dynamic can arise where one person feels responsible for making most of the decisions, which can lead to burnout or frustration if the other party isn't actively involved. Instead of pressuring the partner to make a decision, one could use reverse psychology by saying something like, "I'm sure you don't care much about where we go, so I'll decide this time." This phrase, while it seems like you're relieving the other person of responsibility, could pique their interest and motivate them to be more actively involved in the decision-making, all because they feel like they're choosing of their own free will.

The key to making reverse psychology work in a relationship is to use it carefully and respectfully. It's not about manipulating the other person into doing what we want, but rather understanding how people react when they feel their freedom of choice is being taken away. Most of us want to feel like our decisions are our own, and when we feel like someone else is imposing something on us, it's natural to resist. By using reverse psychology intelligently, we can create a space where the other person feels in control, which can lead to greater cooperation and less conflict.

It is important to mention that reverse psychology should not be the only approach in a relationship. Open communication, mutual respect, and understanding are the foundation of any successful relationship. However, in times of stagnation or when it seems like there is a communication block, reverse psychology can be a useful tool to defuse resistance and allow both parties to come to an agreement. For example, if one person refuses to talk about a sensitive topic, such as financial issues or family decisions, instead of insisting and creating more tension, you could say something like, "I don't think you're ready to talk about this right now, we'll save it for another time." This statement, instead of pushing the conversation, allows the other person to feel less pressured and more willing to open up when they are ready.

One area where reverse psychology can be especially effective is in disagreements about personal changes or habits. Suppose one partner wants the other to quit smoking or adopt healthier habits. Instead of harping on and repeating the same arguments over and over, which can lead to more resistance, you could try something like, "I don't think you're going to quit smoking this year—it's probably too hard for you." This statement can spark in the other person a desire to prove that they are capable of doing so, motivating them to consider a behavior change on their own, without feeling like they're being forced upon.

In long-term relationships, it's common for one partner to want the other to be more involved in the emotional relationship or in day-to-day decision-making. Reverse psychology can be a helpful way to encourage this involvement without the other person feeling obligated. For example, if one person is always the one who organizes weekend outings or activities, they might say something like, "I know you probably don't feel like planning anything this weekend, so I'll do it again." Hearing this might motivate the other person to take the lead, simply to not leave all the responsibility to their partner and to show that they're invested in the relationship, too.

One of the most interesting aspects of reverse psychology in relationships is that it can help change behavior patterns without creating conflict. Many times, when we try to change something about our partner or the dynamics of the relationship, we do it in a very direct way, which creates resistance. By using reverse psychology, we are subtly suggesting the opposite of what we want, allowing the other person to react on their own and make the decision to change. This not only avoids confrontations, but also reinforces the idea that decisions in the relationship are shared and not imposed.

It is important to note that reverse psychology should not be used as a tool to manipulate or control one's partner. Healthy relationships are built on trust, and if one person feels like they are being constantly deceived or manipulated, this can seriously damage the relationship. Reverse psychology should be used sparingly, in specific situations where there is resistance and direct communication does not seem to work. Furthermore, it should be accompanied by honest and open communication, where both parties can express their feelings and needs without fear of being judged.

In summary, reverse psychology can be a valuable tool in relationships when used appropriately. It can help overcome resistance, foster cooperation, and avoid unnecessary conflict. By allowing the other person to feel in control of their decisions, a more harmonious and balanced environment is created in the relationship. However, as with any technique, it is important to use it carefully and respectfully, making sure that the foundation of the relationship remains one of trust and open communication. With the right approach, reverse psychology can be an effective way to improve couple dynamics and strengthen the connection between two people.

Reverse Psychology in Marketing

Reverse psychology is also used very effectively in the world of marketing, where companies seek to influence consumers' purchasing decisions without making them feel like they are being pressured into doing so. In a market saturated with advertising messages, consumers have become more cautious and often react defensively when they feel like they are being sold something directly. This is where reverse psychology comes in: a technique that allows brands to subtly and effectively persuade, making the consumer feel in control of their purchasing decision.

The basic concept of reverse psychology in marketing is to make the customer feel like something is exclusive, limited, or not available to everyone. When people are told that they can't have something or that something is hard to get, they tend to want it even more. This is due to a psychological phenomenon known as "reactance," which is the emotional response that arises when we feel like our freedom of choice is being limited. We want that freedom back, and in the case of marketing, that can lead to consumers wanting to purchase the product that they feel is being taken away or limited.

One of the clearest examples of reverse psychology in marketing is the famous "limited offer" strategy. We often see promotions that say "limited time only" or "few units available." These messages are designed to create a sense of urgency in the consumer, making them feel that if they don't act quickly, they will miss out on the opportunity to purchase the product. Although these types of tactics seem to be designed to restrict access to the product, they are actually increasing the consumer's desire to obtain it. The idea that something is scarce or difficult to obtain makes it more attractive, leading many people to make impulsive purchasing decisions, simply because they fear missing out on the opportunity.

Another way that reverse psychology is applied in marketing is through exclusivity. Luxury brands, for example, often position themselves in such a way that not everyone can afford to buy their products. By doing so, they are not only creating a high-value product, but they are using reverse psychology to make consumers want to be part of that exclusive group that can afford their products. The idea that something is not for everyone, but only for a select group of people, fuels the desire to belong to that group, leading many consumers to aspire to buy luxury products, even if they don't need them or if they are more expensive than they would normally be willing to pay.

The use of reverse psychology in marketing can also be seen in the way brands are presented as "rebels" or "different." Some companies choose to position themselves against traditional market norms or mainstream advertising, sending the message that they are not trying to sell to everyone. For example, a brand may launch a campaign that says, "This product is not for everyone, only for those who truly understand the value of quality." This approach challenges the consumer, making them feel like they must prove that they are part of that special group that "understands" the value of the product, which may lead them to want to buy it to prove that they are sophisticated or knowledgeable enough. In this way, the brand uses reverse psychology to position their products as something desirable, but at the same time seemingly unattainable for some.

Another classic example is the use of the phrase "don't buy it." Some brands have used this approach in their advertising campaigns to surprise the consumer and grab their attention. When a company says "don't buy this product," it immediately grabs attention because it goes against what is expected from a typical advertisement. The strategy here is to make the consumer wonder why they shouldn't buy it, which sparks their curiosity and increases their interest in the product. In many cases, these types of campaigns are designed to highlight a deeper message, such as sustainability or social responsibility, which can also lead to a greater emotional connection with the brand. The end goal remains the same: to attract the consumer and motivate them to make a purchasing decision, but in a way that doesn't seem pushy or pushy.

Digital marketing has also embraced reverse psychology effectively, especially on platforms like social media. Influencers and brands often use phrases like "you probably won't be interested in this, but…" to attract audiences' attention. These types of phrases pique the viewer's curiosity, who may feel like they're missing out on something important by ignoring the message. It's a subtle way to prompt people to engage with content, whether it's watching a video, clicking a link, or purchasing a product. By playing on curiosity and the desire to not be left behind, reverse psychology can lead to increased engagement and participation in content.

In the world of marketing, "exclusive" offers are also a great example of reverse psychology. Often times, brands offer special promotions only to a select group of customers, such as members of a loyalty program. When consumers see that only a specific group can access those offers, they are more motivated to join that group to get the same benefits. These types of strategies make people feel like they are getting something that is not available to everyone, which increases their perception of the value of the product or service. Even when promotions are not as exclusive as they seem, the idea that something is limited or special can strongly influence consumer decision-making.

Reverse psychology can also be effective in marketing innovative or out-of-the-ordinary products. Instead of trying to convince everyone to buy the product, brands can position it as something "too advanced" for the average consumer, creating a challenge. A classic example of this is the marketing of high-end technological devices, where advertisements suggest that only those who truly understand technology will appreciate the product. This approach appeals to consumers who want to see themselves as smart or knowledgeable, motivating them to buy the product to prove that they are up to the challenge.

However, it is important to note that reverse psychology in marketing should be used ethically. While it can be a powerful tool to increase sales, overusing this technique can lead to distrust among consumers. If people feel like they are being constantly manipulated or that limited and exclusive offers are not genuine, they may stop trusting the brand. Therefore, companies need to ensure that the reverse psychology strategies they use are authentic and aligned with the brand's values.

In short, reverse psychology in marketing is an effective technique that taps into people's natural desire to have control over their decisions and to obtain what they perceive as scarce or exclusive. By creating a sense of urgency, exclusivity, or challenge, brands can influence consumers in subtle ways, fostering a desire to buy without making them feel pressured. However, as with any marketing strategy, the key is to use reverse psychology honestly and authentically, so that consumers feel like they are making a conscious and voluntary decision. When used correctly, reverse psychology can be a powerful tool to increase sales and strengthen the emotional connection between brand and consumer.

Alexa Murphy

Reverse Psychology in the Workplace

Reverse psychology in the workplace is a powerful tool that can effectively influence how people react to tasks, challenges, and responsibilities. In the workplace, we are often faced with situations where we need others to do something that might not be within their immediate priorities or that requires extra effort. However, instead of imposing or requiring certain actions, using reverse psychology can motivate employees, colleagues, or even bosses to make proactive decisions and take responsibility voluntarily.

In the workplace, many people tend to resist when they feel they are being pressured or that they have no control over their own actions. This is a common behavior in all areas of life, but at work it can lead to problems with productivity, cooperation, or even create a tense atmosphere. Reverse psychology is based on making the other person feel in control, allowing them to make decisions for themselves rather than feeling forced to act on someone else's instructions. Not only does this improve willingness to complete tasks, but it can also increase motivation and commitment to work.

A clear example of reverse psychology in the workplace can occur when a supervisor needs an employee to perform a task that may be perceived as difficult or undesirable. If the boss approaches in an authoritarian manner and says, "You need to do this now," the employee might react negatively, feeling like an obligation is being imposed on them without their opinion being taken into account. Instead of using this tactic, the supervisor could apply reverse psychology by saying something like, "I know this task is complicated and you probably don't want to do it right now, so we can find someone else to do it." This statement gives the employee a sense of control over the decision, and in many cases, the employee will volunteer to perform the task to prove that they are capable and do not need to be replaced by someone else. By feeling indirectly challenged, the employee can take responsibility with a more positive attitude.

Reverse psychology can also be helpful in managing teams and creating a collaborative environment. Instead of directly assigning tasks to team members, a leader can frame the situation in a way that makes employees feel compelled to take on those responsibilities themselves. For example, instead of saying, "You're handling this project," the leader might say something like, "This project is probably too challenging for you right now—do you want us to find someone else to handle it?" This approach, while appearing to relieve the person of responsibility, actually sparks an internal desire to prove that they can handle the challenge. Instead of feeling forced, the employee may accept the task more willingly and confidently, as they feel like they are choosing to take it on on their own initiative.

Another context where reverse psychology can be effective in the workplace is in meetings or discussions where employees or colleagues are needed to contribute ideas or solutions. Often, people can feel reluctant to participate if they feel their ideas will not be well received or if they feel that too much is expected of them. Instead of insisting that everyone must actively participate, a leader could apply reverse psychology by saying something like, "Not everyone needs to contribute today if they don't have something important to say." This statement can lessen the pressure on employees, making them feel more comfortable sharing their ideas. By not feeling forced to speak, they are more likely to be inspired to do so because they see the opportunity as voluntary rather than imposed.

Reverse psychology can also be applied to change management within a company. When organizations introduce new policies, tools, or working methods, employees may resist the change, especially if they feel they are being forced to adapt. Instead of imposing the change directly, leaders can use reverse psychology to smooth the transition. For example, instead of saying, "Everyone needs to adapt to this new system right away," the message could be, "We know this new system isn't for everyone and some may prefer to stick with the old one, but we're offering it for those who want to explore a more efficient way of working." This approach can spark employees' curiosity and motivate them to try out the new system without feeling pressured, as they perceive it as an option rather than an obligation.

In terms of individual motivation, employees can often benefit from reverse psychology when faced with career goals or challenges. If a leader senses that an employee is losing motivation or not reaching his or her full potential, rather than pressuring the employee to improve his or her performance, he or she can employ reverse psychology by saying something like, "I understand if you're not ready to take on more responsibility right now, you don't have to." This type of feedback can cause the employee to reflect on his or her own capabilities and feel motivated to prove that he or she is capable of taking on a more active role. By presenting the opportunity as optional, the employee can feel more empowered to take action and excel.

Another area where reverse psychology can be effective in the workplace is in making difficult decisions. Often, employees feel uncomfortable making decisions, either because they are afraid of making a mistake or because they do not want to take responsibility for an important decision. In these cases, a leader might say something like, "This decision is probably too complicated for you right now, so I can make it." This statement can gently nudge the employee to reconsider their ability and make the decision themselves—not because they have been asked to, but because they want to prove that they are capable of doing so. By offering the option to relinquish the decision, you create an opportunity for the employee to take the initiative voluntarily.

Reverse psychology can also be helpful in resolving conflicts between colleagues at work. Sometimes people resist apologizing or reaching an agreement when they feel the need to do so is being forced upon them. Instead of demanding that two employees resolve their differences, a supervisor might say, "I don't think it's necessary for you to sit down and talk about this right now—it's probably not the best time." This statement can ease initial tension and allow both parties to feel like they have control over the conflict resolution process, which can lead to more voluntary and effective reconciliation.

However, as with any psychological technique, it is important to use reverse psychology sparingly and ethically in the workplace. Overusing this technique can lead to distrust among employees or even create a hostile work environment if people feel they are being constantly manipulated. It is crucial that leaders and supervisors use reverse psychology in a respectful manner, ensuring that the end goal is to improve team motivation, productivity, and well-being, and not simply force people to do something they do not want to do.

In short, reverse psychology is a powerful tool that, when applied correctly, can transform the dynamics in the workplace. By giving people the feeling that they have control over their decisions, a greater sense of autonomy and motivation can be fostered. Employees feel more engaged and willing to take responsibility when they perceive that they are making decisions on their own, rather than being forced to do so. The key is to use reverse psychology ethically and carefully, always with the goal of creating a positive and collaborative work environment.

The Risks of Reverse Psychology

Reverse psychology can be an effective tool in many situations, but like any technique, it also carries risks if not used properly. While it is tempting to think that it will always work to get people to do what we want, it is important to remember that we are dealing with the emotions, thoughts, and decisions of others. Manipulating these aspects incorrectly or excessively can have negative consequences that affect both personal and professional relationships. In this chapter, we will explore the potential risks of using reverse psychology and why it is critical to use it carefully and consciously.

One of the main risks of reverse psychology is that it can create distrust. When people realize they are being manipulated, they may feel deceived or betrayed. This is especially true if the technique is used repeatedly or in situations where people perceive that they are not being spoken to directly. No one wants to feel like a piece in a game where the rules are not clear. In relationships, whether at work, with friends or with family, trust is essential, and if it is broken due to manipulation, it can be very difficult to regain.

For example, if you consistently use reverse psychology on a colleague at work to get them to take on tasks they don't want to do, they may eventually catch on to the strategy. At that point, they might start to question all interactions and motivations, wondering if they're being manipulated in other areas as well. This lack of trust can damage the working relationship and even affect team dynamics if other people also start to perceive that things aren't being handled transparently. Instead of creating an environment of cooperation, misused reverse psychology can foster distrust and a lack of commitment.

Another significant risk is that reverse psychology can lead to the opposite of the intended effect. People don't always react the way we expect, and in some cases, they might simply take our words at face value and act accordingly. For example, if you tell someone that "you probably can't do this," hoping that will motivate them to try, they might simply respond, "You're right, I can't," and decide to do nothing. Instead of motivating the person, you would have reinforced their sense of inability. This can happen in anything from parenting to teamwork. Instead of empowering people to try hard, inappropriate use of reverse psychology could cause them to become discouraged and shy away from challenges.

In personal relationships, this risk is particularly high. If a partner tries to use reverse psychology to get the other person to do something, they may end up causing a negative reaction. For example, if one partner says something like, "I don't think you care enough to do this for me," the other person might feel hurt or resentful rather than motivated to prove otherwise. Instead of strengthening the relationship, reverse psychology could lead to unnecessary tension, distance, or arguments. This risk is magnified when deep emotions are involved, as people tend to be more sensitive when it comes to personal relationships.

Another important aspect to consider is that reverse psychology can be seen as a form of emotional manipulation. Although sometimes the intentions may be good, if someone feels emotionally manipulated, the reaction can be quite negative. No one wants to feel controlled or as if their decisions are being deceptively influenced. In this sense, reverse psychology could cross the line between persuasion and manipulation, which can have serious consequences for relationships. People may feel humiliated or disrespected if they feel that their emotions are being used against them to make them act a certain way.

It is crucial to note that reverse psychology is not a magic solution to solving problems or conflicts. It should not be seen as a strategy that we resort to every time we do not get what we want from others. If used too often, it can lose its effectiveness and become predictable. When people realize that you are always trying to manipulate them in this way, they may simply stop reacting or become resistant to any kind of request. Instead of motivating them, you could end up making people less cooperative and more defensive.

In the workplace, misuse of reverse psychology can seriously damage team morale. If leaders use this technique to get employees to take on tasks or responsibilities they don't want, workers may feel exploited or manipulated. In the long term, this can lead to demotivation and resentment. A work team where people feel they are being manipulated is not a well-functioning team or one that is committed to common goals. Leadership should be based on trust, transparency, and open communication, not psychological tactics that, while they may be effective in the short term, can erode team well-being over time.

In more sensitive situations, such as parenting, misapplied reverse psychology can have long-lasting effects on children's emotional development. If parents consistently use this technique to manipulate their children's behavior, children may learn to react in a defiant manner or develop a distrustful attitude toward authority. They may also feel insecure about when they are being told the truth or when they are being manipulated, which can affect their ability to trust the people who should be caring for and guiding them. Parenting based on manipulation can lead to problems in the parent-child relationship and make it difficult to develop honest and open communication.

On the other hand, there is the risk that some people may not react with distrust, but with resentment or anger. If they feel they are being manipulated into doing something they do not want, they might respond with hostility or simply ignore any attempts at persuasion. Such reactions can make the situation worse rather than solving it, and lead to unnecessary conflict. In extreme cases, it could seriously damage personal or work relationships, leaving a feeling of awkwardness or tension instead of cooperation.

Finally, a major risk that is often overlooked is the impact on the person using reverse psychology. When someone employs this technique frequently, they may develop a dependency on indirect manipulation rather than learning to communicate their needs and desires clearly and directly. This can lead to a lack of assertive communication skills and a pattern of dysfunctional relationships, where manipulation becomes the norm rather than the exception. In the long run, this can be detrimental to personal growth and healthy relationships.

In conclusion, while reverse psychology can be a useful and effective technique in some situations, it also carries significant risks that should be considered. Using it inappropriately or excessively can lead to mistrust, resentment, and other negative effects in both personal and professional relationships. The key to avoiding these risks is to use reverse psychology sparingly, always with respect for the feelings and decisions of others, and to be aware that it is not always the best solution. Human relationships require honesty, transparency, and clear communication, and while reverse psychology can be useful at certain times, it should not become an everyday tool or a substitute for sincere communication.

Reverse Psychology and Self-Esteem

Reverse psychology can have a profound impact on self-esteem, both positively and negatively, depending on how it is used. Self-esteem, which refers to a person's perception and value of themselves, is a crucial part of our emotional well-being. When we interact with others, especially in situations where we are trying to influence their decisions or behaviors, it is important to consider how our words and actions can affect that person's self-esteem. In this chapter, we will explore the relationship between reverse psychology and self-esteem, how it can influence it, and the implications this has on everyday relationships.

To understand this relationship, it's helpful to think about how reverse psychology works on an emotional level. Reverse psychology involves saying the opposite of what we really want someone to do, with the expectation that the person will react in a way that is contrary to what we've said. For example, if you tell a friend that you don't think they're capable of achieving something, in the hope that this will motivate them to try the opposite, you're using reverse psychology. However, how that person perceives your words can have a significant impact on their self-esteem.

If the person has healthy self-esteem, reverse psychology is likely to work in the expected way. Hearing that they don't believe they are capable of doing something can trigger their desire to prove otherwise, giving them additional motivation to achieve their goals. In this case, the person may interpret the comment as a challenge that reinforces their confidence in their abilities. As they face the challenge and achieve their goal, their self-esteem may be strengthened, as they will feel more capable and confident in themselves. In these cases, reverse psychology can be a boost to personal growth and self-esteem.

However, when a person's self-esteem is fragile or low, reverse psychology can have a negative effect. Instead of feeling motivated by the challenge, the person might interpret the comment as criticism or validation of their own insecurities. For example, if someone is already feeling insecure about their abilities to complete a task and they hear someone else say that they don't think they can do it, instead of challenging themselves, they might give up and further convince themselves that they really aren't capable. Instead of acting as a catalyst for action, reverse psychology in this case reinforces the negative beliefs the person already has about themselves, which can further weaken their self-esteem.

It's important to remember that self-esteem is a very sensitive thing. Many people struggle with their own doubts and fears, and what may seem like a simple motivational strategy can end up hurting someone if not used carefully. Instead of motivating a person, you could be feeding into their insecurities or even leading them to avoid the challenge altogether. This is especially true in situations where the relationship between people is hierarchical in nature, such as between parents and children, teachers and students, or bosses and employees. In these cases, the person receiving the comment may feel like their worth is being questioned by someone in a position of authority, which can have an even deeper impact on their self-esteem.

Furthermore, repeated use of reverse psychology can lead to an erosion of self-esteem over time. If a person is constantly exposed to negative feedback that, while well-intentioned, is designed to motivate them through challenge, they might start to internalize that criticism. Instead of seeing it as a drive to improve, they might start to believe that others actually think they are not capable. This accumulation of negative feedback can lead to a gradual deterioration of self-esteem, especially if there is no positive reinforcement to balance out the criticism. In the long term, this can affect a person's confidence in their own abilities, leading them to avoid challenging situations out of fear of failure.

In this regard, reverse psychology should be used with caution, especially when dealing with people with low self-esteem. Rather than using strategies that involve negative challenge, it may be more beneficial to focus on positive reinforcement and validation of the person's capabilities. Telling someone that you are confident in their ability to do something or highlighting their past achievements can be a much more effective way of boosting their self-esteem and motivating them to take on new challenges. When people feel supported and valued, they are more likely to feel safe to take risks and try new things, which in turn strengthens their self-esteem.

Another important consideration is how reverse psychology affects our own self-esteem. Sometimes, people who frequently use reverse psychology do so because they feel they cannot communicate effectively or directly. Instead of expressing their needs or desires clearly, they resort to indirect manipulation, which may reflect a lack of confidence in their ability to influence others in an overt manner. In the long term, this reliance on reverse psychology can erode the self-esteem of the person using it, as they may feel unable to handle interpersonal situations without resorting to psychological tactics.

In relationships, reverse psychology can also affect the self-esteem of both parties. If one person feels like they are constantly being manipulated through negative comments or challenges, they may begin to question not only their own worth, but also the quality of the relationship. Healthy relationships are built on open communication, trust, and mutual support. If one person perceives that the other is trying to manipulate them or that they don't trust their abilities, this can damage the relationship and affect the self-esteem of both.

Finally, it's important to recognize that reverse psychology isn't the only tool available to motivate people or influence their behavior. In many cases, the best way to boost someone's self-esteem is through direct, honest, and positive communication. When people feel valued, heard, and understood, their self-esteem naturally grows. Instead of trying to manipulate someone into doing what you want, you can motivate people by reminding them of their worth and ability to overcome challenges.

In short, reverse psychology can have a significant impact on self-esteem, both positively and negatively. While it can be helpful in certain situations, especially with people who have healthy self-esteem, it can also be detrimental to those who already struggle with insecurities. It's critical to use this technique with caution, be aware of how our words and actions can affect others, and remember that positive reinforcement and open communication are often far more effective at building self-esteem and encouraging personal growth.

Reverse Psychology and Decision Making

Decision making is a fundamental process in our lives. Every day, without realizing it, we make dozens or even hundreds of decisions, from the simplest ones like what clothes to wear, to more complex decisions that can have a significant impact on our future, such as changing jobs or moving to another city. In this process, reverse psychology can play an important role, as it can influence the way people make decisions. In this chapter, we will explore how reverse psychology affects the decision-making process, why it works in certain contexts, and what its potential limitations are.

When we talk about making decisions, we are talking about a cognitive process in which we evaluate different options and choose one. However, the interesting thing is that we do not always make decisions in a completely rational way. Our emotions, impulses, previous experiences and, of course, external influences play a crucial role in this process. Reverse psychology is based precisely on taking advantage of some of these influences to guide a person towards a certain decision, but in an indirect way.

The fundamental principle behind reverse psychology in decision-making is that when a person is told to do something, especially if they feel like they are being controlled or limited in their options, their natural reaction is to want to do the opposite. This has to do with our innate need for autonomy and control over our own lives. We want to feel like our decisions are our own, that we are free to choose, and that no one else is dictating what we should do. That's why when someone tells us "don't do that" or "I don't think you can pull that off," we often feel the urge to try the opposite, even if we hadn't initially considered that option.

This phenomenon can be clearly seen in everyday situations. Imagine someone telling you that you shouldn't take a certain course because it's too difficult for you. Even if you hadn't thought about taking it before, the idea that someone is questioning your abilities might make you reconsider that choice just to prove that you are capable. In some way, the negative comment triggers an internal desire to reassert your independence and abilities. This is reverse psychology in action. It's not that the person actually wants you to choose that choice, but rather, by telling you that you can't or shouldn't, they're prompting you to consider the possibility that you can and should.

In decision making, this mechanism can be useful in a variety of situations. A classic example is when parents are trying to get their children to make responsible decisions. Instead of simply imposing a rule or forbidding something, parents can suggest that the child do the opposite of what they actually want them to do. For example, if a parent wants their child to finish their homework before going out to play, instead of saying "do your homework first," they might say something like "you can go play if you really don't mind getting bad grades." This type of comment causes the child to reflect on the situation and possibly decide on their own to do the homework first to avoid negative consequences, feeling that it was their own decision.

The interesting thing about reverse psychology in decision making is that often people are not aware that they are being influenced. They believe they are making an autonomous decision, when in fact they have been guided towards that choice. This can be advantageous in certain circumstances, but it also raises ethical questions about manipulation. It is important to note that reverse psychology should be used sparingly and in situations where it truly benefits the person and not just the person doing it. Constantly manipulating the decisions of others can erode trust and damage relationships.

Despite its effectiveness in some situations, reverse psychology has limitations in decision making, especially when it comes to more complex decisions. It is not always a guarantee of success. If a person is aware that they are being manipulated, they might deliberately resist and do the opposite, not out of defiance, but to maintain control over their own decision. Also, if a person is very sure of what they want or has a strong conviction about a particular choice, reverse psychology will probably not have much of an effect. In those cases, people are less influenced by what others tell them to do or not to do.

An interesting example is marketing, where reverse psychology is used to influence consumer purchasing decisions. In this context, companies may suggest that a product is exclusive or hard to get, knowing that consumers often want what seems difficult to obtain. Phrases like "this product isn't for everyone" or "you may not need this, but…" create the feeling that the consumer must make a decision for themselves, and in many cases, that decision is to go for the product. The desire not to miss out on something exclusive or to prove that they can access something that seems limited drives the purchase decision.

On a personal level, reverse psychology can also be used to influence decisions related to behavior and relationships. For example, in a friendship or romantic relationship, one person might use reverse psychology to get the other party to make a decision that they might not have otherwise considered. Imagine someone saying, "You probably don't want to come to this dinner because it's not something you're interested in," when they actually expect the other person to go. By suggesting that participation is not expected, they might spark a desire to be present and participate in the activity, leading to a decision that is contrary to the initial suggestion.

It is important to mention that reverse psychology is not always the best tool to influence decision making, especially when it comes to long-term or high-stakes decisions. In these cases, it is essential to promote informed and thoughtful decision making. Guiding someone towards a decision simply by using a psychological trick may be effective in the short term, but if all options have not been properly evaluated, the decision may not be the most beneficial one. Furthermore, important decisions require time to be analyzed, and a subtle influence like reverse psychology could lead to an impulsive choice.

In the workplace, for example, reverse psychology could be applied to motivate an employee to take the lead on a project. A boss might say, "I'm not sure you're ready to lead this project yet," which could make the employee feel motivated to prove otherwise. However, if used inappropriately or consistently, it can create an environment of manipulation rather than trust, which can negatively impact morale and workplace culture.

In short, reverse psychology can be a powerful tool in decision-making, taking advantage of our natural tendency to want to assert our autonomy and challenge the expectations of others. When used carefully and with good intentions, it can help guide people towards decisions they might not otherwise have considered. However, it is important to recognize its limitations and the risks of its misuse. Decision-making is a complex process, and while reverse psychology can be useful in certain situations, it should not be seen as a magic solution. The key is to use it sparingly and in situations where it can truly benefit the person making the decision, always respecting their ability to choose for themselves.

How to Spot Reverse Psychology

Spotting reverse psychology can seem challenging at first, because this technique relies on the person not being aware that they are being manipulated. Reverse psychology is, by nature, subtle and often goes unnoticed. However, with a little practice and attention, it is possible to identify when someone is trying to influence your decisions indirectly. In this chapter, we will explore how to recognize the signs of reverse psychology, why some people use it, and how you can respond effectively when you realize that someone is trying to influence you in this way.

The first step in spotting reverse psychology is to develop a heightened awareness of how other people talk to you and what they're actually saying. Often, reverse psychology manifests itself when someone suggests you do the opposite of what they actually expect you to do. For example, if someone tells you, "You probably don't want to go out tonight, you'd probably rather stay in," when they clearly want you to go out, this is a classic form of reverse psychology. The person is counting on your need to assert your independence to lead you to choose to go out, even if you hadn't considered it before.

One of the keys to spotting reverse psychology is to pay attention to the emotions that the other person's comments stir in you. If you notice that a comment triggers an immediate impulse to do the opposite of what they're suggesting, it may be a sign that you're being subjected to reverse psychology. People who use this technique often rely on our natural tendency to react defensively when we feel that someone is questioning our decisions or abilities. For example, if someone says, "You sure can't do that, it's too hard for you," and you suddenly feel the urge to prove that you can do it, you may very well be being manipulated through reverse psychology.

Another way to spot reverse psychology is to look at whether the person often uses belittling or defiance tactics. Often, reverse psychology relies on making someone feel challenged or belittled in subtle ways, which triggers a reaction to prove otherwise. If someone often tells you things like, "I don't think that's something you can handle," or "that doesn't seem like it would be in your best interest," when you actually know that person would want you to do that, they are probably trying to influence your decision in a reverse way. These defiance tactics appeal to our pride and desire to prove our capabilities.

Reverse psychology can also be detected when the other person's communication seems contradictory. For example, imagine that a friend invites you to a party, but says "I don't really think you'll have fun, you'd probably rather stay home." In this case, although they are suggesting that you don't go, they may actually want you to reconsider. This contradiction between what they say and what they actually want can be a clear sign that they are using reverse psychology. It is important to note that often, those who use this technique prefer not to openly express their true desires, so their words tend to be more indirect or ambiguous.

It's also helpful to look at the context in which the conversation is taking place. Situations where there is a desire for control or influence over decisions tend to be more conducive to the use of reverse psychology. For example, parents sometimes use this tactic with their children when they want them to follow certain rules or make good decisions, but without imposing them in an authoritarian manner. Instead of saying, "You should do your homework," they might say, "It doesn't matter if you don't do your homework, you probably don't need good grades for your future." This strategy puts the child in a position where they feel they must challenge the suggestion in order to make a better decision. If you sense that someone is trying to influence you, especially when it comes to important decisions, it may be a sign that they are using reverse psychology.

Another aspect to consider is how the other person handles power in the interaction. People who use reverse psychology tend to take a passive or seemingly disinterested stance, while in reality they are very invested in the outcome of the decision. If someone who clearly cares about a decision suddenly seems very unconcerned or acts like they don't care what you choose, they may be trying to influence your decision in an indirect way. This tactic may create a sense of freedom in the other person, but it is actually designed to guide them toward a specific choice.

One of the most effective ways to spot reverse psychology is to ask direct questions. If you sense that someone is trying to influence you, you can ask them outright what their true opinion is or what they really expect you to do. By confronting ambiguity or indirection with a clear question, you can force the other person to be honest about their intentions. For example, if someone says to you, "I don't think you can handle this project, but if you want to try, go ahead," you might respond with something like, "Do you think I really can't do it, or are you just testing me?" This strategy can expose the use of reverse psychology while also helping you make a decision based on clearer information.

Once you detect that someone is using reverse psychology, it's important to think about how you want to react. It's not always necessary to resist the influence. Sometimes, the person using this technique has good intentions and is trying to motivate you in a way that, although indirect, can be helpful. For example, if someone is trying to challenge you to do something that benefits you, such as taking on a new challenge or improving a skill, you might decide that this influence is positive and choose to go ahead with the action. However, if you feel that the manipulation is harmful or that the other person is trying to control your decisions without being sincere, you might choose to confront the situation directly or simply not fall into the trap of doing the opposite of what they tell you.

Another important point is to understand why people resort to reverse psychology. Often, they do so because they feel they cannot influence decisions directly, or because they believe that by telling you what they really want, they might face resistance. In many cases, these people are trying to avoid conflict or open confrontation, so they resort to more subtle tactics. In other cases, it may be a power dynamic where the person wants to maintain a position of control over the situation without appearing too dominant. Understanding these motivations can help you respond more clearly and handle the situation in a more balanced way.

Reverse psychology can also be present in the media and advertising. Advertising messages often use this technique to influence our purchasing decisions or to guide our behavior as consumers. Phrases such as "it's not for everyone" or "you probably don't need it" may be attempts to spark your desire to purchase a product or service by suggesting that it is exclusive or difficult to obtain. In these cases, being aware of how these tactics are used in the commercial environment will help you make more informed and less impulsive decisions.

In short, reverse psychology can be difficult to spot because it relies on subtle tactics and indirect influences. However, by paying attention to contradictory comments, the emotions they generate, and the context of the conversation, you can begin to notice when someone is trying to manipulate your decisions in this way. Asking direct questions and reflecting on the other person's true intentions can also help you expose the use of reverse psychology and make more conscious and autonomous decisions. The key is to be aware of your own reactions and not be carried away by impulses that have been generated by external influences.

Real Cases

Throughout history, reverse psychology has found applications in a variety of areas of daily life, from parenting to marketing, the workplace, and personal relationships. In this chapter, we will explore some real-life cases that illustrate how reverse psychology has been used to influence people's decisions and behaviors. By looking at concrete examples, we can better understand how this technique can be effective and, in some cases, unexpectedly powerful.

One of the most common examples of reverse psychology occurs in the realm of parenting. Parents, in their desire to guide their children toward correct choices, often resort to this tactic without even realizing it. A typical case is that of a child who refuses to eat his vegetables. Instead of insisting that the child eat them, which can increase resistance, a parent can say something like, "I don't think you want to eat those vegetables, you probably don't like them." This comment can spark the child's curiosity or desire to challenge the suggestion, and he will most likely end up eating them just to prove that he can. Although this example seems simple, it shows how reverse psychology can trigger an unexpected reaction when someone feels in control of their decision.

A more elaborate example is found in the world of marketing. Companies and advertisers have perfected the use of reverse psychology to influence consumer decisions. In the 1990s, a famous Coca-Cola campaign in Japan used this technique brilliantly. Instead of promoting their product as something that everyone should have, they built a campaign around the idea that "Coke is not for everyone." The phrase suggested that only really special or select people would enjoy the product, which triggered a desire in consumers to belong to that exclusive group. Instead of rejecting the product, consumers were drawn to it because of this implied exclusivity. This campaign was a huge success and shows how reverse psychology can be used on a large scale to influence the masses.

An even more fascinating case occurred in military history. During World War II, the

Allies used a form of reverse psychology in their disinformation tactics. They knew that the Germans were intercepting their communications, so they began transmitting false information suggesting that a key attack would take place in a certain location, while the real attack was planned somewhere else. By making the Germans believe that they had discovered secret information, they actually tricked them into preparing their defenses in the wrong place. This disinformation tactic was extremely effective, as it took advantage of the enemy's desire to act in ways contrary to what they perceived as "the trap." This is a clear example of how reverse psychology, although subtle, can have an enormous impact even in critical scenarios such as war.

Another interesting case is that of the famous American psychologist BF Skinner, who used a version of reverse psychology in his experiments on human behavior. Skinner was known for his work on operant conditioning, and in one of his experiments, he placed a pigeon in a box with a lever that released food only when the pigeon did not press the lever. Instead of teaching the pigeon to press the lever to get food, as would be expected, the bird was conditioned to avoid the action, achieving the opposite result. This experiment shows how, at a basic level, living beings can be trained to act in ways contrary to what might be expected, demonstrating that reverse psychology is not only applicable to humans, but also has broader foundations in the nature of behavior.

In the workplace, reverse psychology has also proven to be useful. One famous case is that of Steve Jobs, co-founder of Apple, who often used this technique to motivate his employees to reach their full potential. Jobs had a very particular way of leading his team, and he would often challenge his engineers by telling them that a task was "impossible" or that he didn't think they could do it in the required time. This strategy, which might seem demotivating, actually drove his team to prove Jobs wrong, and as a result, they managed to complete seemingly impossible tasks in record time. Although he was not always appreciated for his leadership style, Jobs' ability to use reverse psychology motivated many of his employees to perform above their own expectations.

In personal relationships, reverse psychology has also played a significant role. An interesting case occurred in a couple who had been arguing about the organization of their home. The husband was constantly complaining that his wife left her things in a mess and did not put enough effort into keeping the house organized. Instead of arguing about the issue any further, the husband decided to use reverse psychology. One day, instead of insisting that the wife organize her things, he began to praise her for being "so carefree and creative" that she did not mind the mess. By doing this, the wife, who previously felt criticized and controlled, began to feel the urge to prove that she could be organized as well. Without the husband mentioning it again, she began to organize the house on her own, proving that reverse psychology, in the right context, can change behaviors without the need for direct confrontation.

Finally, a real-life case that many people have experienced is the use of reverse psychology in sales. Salespeople often employ this technique when trying to convince an undecided customer. A car salesperson, for example, might say "I don't think this car is right for you, you probably want something simpler." This type of comment can make the customer, instead of walking away, feel challenged and decide to consider the car they were initially ruling out. Not only does this approach make the customer feel in control of their decision, but it also creates the illusion that they are making an independent decision, when in fact they have been subtly influenced by the salesperson.

In short, real-life cases of reverse psychology are varied and appear in multiple facets of everyday life. Whether in parenting, marketing, personal relationships, or even in scenarios as complex as war, this technique has proven effective in influencing human behavior. The interesting thing about reverse psychology is that often the person being influenced does not realize that they are acting according to someone else's wishes. Instead, they feel that they are making a free and autonomous decision. The key to making reverse psychology work lies in its subtlety and the ability to play on a person's emotions and desire for control.

Alexa Murphy

Reverse Psychology in Advertising and Media

Reverse psychology is a powerful tool used not only in personal interactions, but also in advertising and the media. Companies and advertisers have learned to use it to influence consumer decisions in subtle and often imperceptible ways. Instead of directly telling you to buy a product or subscribe to a service, advertisements often suggest the opposite or employ tactics that appeal to our desire for independence and autonomy. This approach works because when we feel that something is forbidden or discouraged, we tend to desire it more. In this chapter, we will explore how reverse psychology is used in advertising and the media to capture our attention and direct our purchasing decisions.

One of the first principles of reverse psychology in advertising is the use of exclusivity. Over the years, brands have learned that by suggesting that a product is "not for everyone" or is only available to a select group, many people will want to get it just to feel part of that special group. A classic example is a well-known luxury car brand's slogan that read "Not everyone can drive a [brand name]." This message doesn't directly say "buy this car," but instead puts forward the idea that only people with certain qualities, such as success or good taste, should have access to it. As a result, people who want to be seen as part of that elite feel the need to acquire the car to demonstrate their status, even though they weren't explicitly asked to do so.

Another common example of reverse psychology in advertising is when brands use "lightning" to create an unexpected desire in consumers. Instead of highlighting the product's outstanding features or pressuring the audience to buy it, some brands choose to do the opposite, downplaying the need to purchase it. This is often seen in campaigns targeting young people, where the message is something like "you probably don't need this product." By doing so, brands pique consumer curiosity and get them to want to try the product simply because it doesn't seem to be being pushed in a pushy way. This approach makes consumers feel like they are making the decision for themselves, when in fact they have been subtly influenced by the advertising campaign.

The media has also adopted reverse psychology in many of its strategies. An obvious example is when access to certain information is banned or restricted. When the media suggests that something is "too controversial" or "not suitable for all audiences," many people feel an immediate need to watch or listen to what is being censored or restricted. This is due to a psychological phenomenon known as the "reactance effect," which occurs when a person perceives that their freedom of choice is being threatened, generating an almost automatic impulse to regain that freedom by taking the action they are being suggested to avoid. In this sense, the media can use reverse psychology to generate interest in certain programs or news, simply by implying that they are not for everyone.

A real-life example of reverse psychology in the media occurred during the promotion of the film "The Blair Witch." Instead of selling it as a conventional horror film, the creators opted for a marketing campaign that suggested the film was a real documentary about mysterious events. The campaign played on doubt and ambiguity, suggesting that "it might not be for everyone" because the material was too intense or disturbing. This approach attracted a large number of people who wanted to see if they could handle the film, fueling their curiosity about what seemed forbidden or exclusive. In the end, the film was a resounding success, largely due to the campaign's ability to spark interest that otherwise would not have existed.

Another more modern example of reverse psychology in advertising is the use of "scarcity." Many online stores and retail platforms use messages like "only 2 left" or "limited time offer," which induce consumers to act quickly. Even though most of the time these products will be available again later, the fact that the consumer feels like they are about to miss out on the opportunity to buy something triggers an immediate reaction. This type of message plays on our need to not miss out on something valuable or special, and pushes us to make quick purchasing decisions based on the subtle pressure of scarcity. This technique actually takes advantage of reverse psychology, as instead of directly saying "buy now," they are indirectly telling you that if you don't, you will miss out on something important.

Social media is also a fertile field for reverse psychology. Influencers, for example, often use this technique when promoting products or services. Instead of telling their audience that they need to buy something, they can use phrases like "it's probably not for everyone" or "only the truly interested will understand why I use this." These statements create a sense of exclusivity and provoke followers' desire to be part of that small "select" group that dares to try what is being promoted. By presenting it as something not necessary or not suitable for everyone, influencers manage to make their followers feel more attracted to the product, since no one wants to feel excluded or left out of something that seems interesting.

In the realm of entertainment, reverse psychology also features prominently. TV series, books, or even video games often use anticipation tactics to generate interest. For example, when a movie is labeled "the scariest of the year" but is also said to be "not for everyone," fans of the genre feel an immediate need to test whether they can actually handle it. This approach is also common in video games, where promotional campaigns sometimes include messages suggesting that the game is "too difficult for most." These indirect messages challenge players to prove their skill, creating extra motivation to purchase and try the game, driven by the desire to prove they can overcome the challenge.

Furthermore, reverse psychology is not only used in advertising for products or entertainment, it is also seen in social and political campaigns. In many public health campaigns, for example, messages may suggest that a negative behavior is something that most people would probably not want to change, causing people to go out of their way to prove that they are not in that group. For example, in campaigns to reduce tobacco use, instead of directly saying "quit smoking," you might see ads that say "most people think quitting smoking is too hard," which pushes some smokers to want to prove otherwise and overcome that challenge.

In short, reverse psychology is a strategy widely used in advertising and media to influence consumer decisions and behaviors. By suggesting the opposite of what is actually desired, it arouses the consumer's desire to act against the initial suggestion, driven by the need to feel independent, defy expectations, or not miss out on something important. Brands, media, and influencers have perfected this technique, using it to capture our attention and direct our decisions in an indirect but very effective way. Understanding how this strategy works can help us become more conscious consumers and less susceptible to the subtle manipulation that surrounds us in our daily lives.

Reverse Psychology in Personal Development

Reverse psychology, though commonly associated with external manipulation, can also be a powerful tool in the realm of personal development. In the context of individual growth, reverse psychology can be used to help us overcome internal obstacles, such as self-sabotage, procrastination, and self-imposed limitations. By learning to apply this technique to ourselves, we can change the way we approach our goals and challenges, giving us a new perspective on how to motivate ourselves more effectively. Though it may seem paradoxical, using reverse psychology in personal development can be an eye-opening strategy for improving our lives.

One of the main ways that reverse psychology can be applied in personal development is in dealing with procrastination. We have all experienced times when, despite having an important task to do, we find a thousand and one ways to distract ourselves and put it off. Instead of fighting that impulse to procrastinate, we can use reverse psychology to turn the situation around. For example, if you have a task due that you keep avoiding, instead of telling yourself "I should do it now," you could tell yourself "I probably don't want to do it now, maybe I should wait for later." This approach may surprise you, as by giving your mind permission not to do it, an opposite reaction can arise: suddenly, you find yourself motivated to start the task because you no longer feel forced to do it. The trick is to challenge your own internal resistance in a way that takes the pressure off you, which often reduces the desire to avoid the task.

Another interesting use of reverse psychology in personal development is in dealing with self-sabotage. Self-sabotage occurs when we consciously or unconsciously make decisions that go against our own best interests, often out of fear of failure or success. A common example is when we are about to start an important project, but instead of moving forward, we find excuses not to start. In these cases, instead of punishing yourself for your actions, you could apply reverse psychology by telling yourself something like "it's better not to start this project because it will probably fail anyway." By saying this, your mind may react in unexpected ways, prompting you to prove otherwise and take action. The key here is to gently challenge the limiting belief, which can break the cycle of self-sabotage and make you more inclined to act.

Reverse psychology can also be helpful when it comes to developing new habits. Imagine you're trying to adopt a healthy habit, such as exercising regularly. Instead of forcing yourself to stick to a strict routine or feeling guilty for not sticking to it, you could use reverse psychology in a gentle way. You could tell yourself something like, "I don't need to go to the gym today, it probably won't make much difference if I do it tomorrow." This type of thinking, while it may seem like it's undermining your goal, can actually make you feel less pressured and therefore more inclined to go to the gym without feeling forced. Reverse psychology, when used in this context, can help you create a more relaxed mental space, where you don't feel guilty about every decision, which in turn can increase your motivation.

A fascinating aspect of reverse psychology in personal development is its impact on self-image. Often, when we are working on improving our lives, we face moments of self-doubt where we don't believe we are capable of achieving our goals. In these moments, using reverse psychology can be transformative. For example, if you are faced with negative thoughts such as "I'll never be good enough at this," you might respond to yourself in an ironic or contrary way: "I may not be the best at this, but that doesn't matter." By doing so, you are playing into the beliefs that are limiting you, challenging them in a non-confrontational way. Instead of fighting your own negative thoughts head-on, you are approaching them from a different angle, which can help you reduce the emotional impact these thoughts have on you.

Reverse psychology can also be applied to making difficult decisions. Often, when faced with an important decision, we can feel overwhelmed by the fear of making a mistake or taking the wrong path. In these cases, instead of putting pressure on yourself to make the right decision, you might tell yourself something like, "No matter what decision I make, it probably won't change much." This approach de-dramatizes the situation, which can relieve internal pressure and allow you to make the decision without feeling trapped in anxiety. By taking the weight off the importance of the decision, your mind relaxes and you can think more clearly. Reverse psychology, in this sense, becomes a tool to relieve the stress and fear associated with important decisions, giving you the freedom to act with more confidence.

In the context of personal development, it is also important to understand that reverse psychology is not about tricking ourselves or manipulating our emotions in negative ways. Rather, it is about playing with our internal expectations and breaking patterns of thinking that limit us. Often, our biggest obstacles are internal, and reverse psychology can help us see our resistances from a different angle. In doing so, we can find creative solutions to problems and unlock parts of ourselves that previously seemed inaccessible. This can lead to deeper personal growth and greater self-understanding.

Applying reverse psychology can also be helpful in breaking cycles of repetitive or negative thinking. Often times when we are stuck in a cycle of negativity, trying to get out of it directly only reinforces it. If, for example, you are stuck in a thought like "I will never be able to improve," you might respond with something like "maybe not, and that's okay, not everyone can improve." By accepting the possibility of not improving, the mind no longer feels the need to resist it as much, and this relief of pressure can result in you finding more strength to keep going.

In short, reverse psychology is a versatile tool that can be applied effectively in personal development. Whether it is to overcome procrastination, self-sabotage or limiting beliefs, this technique offers us a new way to face ourselves and our challenges. Instead of forcing ourselves to meet rigid expectations or fighting our own negative thoughts, reverse psychology allows us to adopt a more relaxed attitude, where pressure decreases and motivation naturally increases. By learning to apply this strategy in our daily lives, we can unlock smoother and more effective personal growth, allowing us to move forward with less resistance and more confidence in our abilities.

Ethics and Limits of Reverse Psychology

Reverse psychology can be a powerful tool, and like any tool that has a great impact on people, its use should be guided by ethical principles. When we talk about ethics, we are referring to the rules and values that help us discern what is right and what is wrong, especially in situations where our actions affect others. Although reverse psychology can be very useful in various contexts, such as parenting, marketing, or personal development, it is important to ask: when is its use appropriate? Is there a limit to manipulating people? In this chapter, we will explore the ethical implications of using reverse psychology and set some boundaries that should be respected so that its use is not harmful or manipulative.

First, it is crucial to understand that reverse psychology, at its core, involves a form of manipulation. By telling someone the opposite of what you want them to do, with the intention of getting them to act against your suggestion, you are influencing their behavior without them explicitly knowing it. This raises an important question: is it ethical to manipulate people, even if it is for their own benefit? For example, a parent might use reverse psychology to convince their child to do something that is good for them, such as studying or eating healthy. In this case, the end goal is positive, but a manipulative tactic is still being used. Even if the intention is good, the fact that the other person is not aware that they are being influenced can be a cause for concern. This is where ethics come into play: the use of reverse psychology should be limited by respect for the other person's autonomy.

One crucial aspect to consider is transparency. While reverse psychology can be effective, using it constantly can lead to distrust. People, especially in close relationships, value honesty. If someone finds out that you have been using reverse psychology to influence their decisions, they might feel that you have not been honest or that you have played with their emotions. This can negatively affect relationships, as trust is one of the fundamental pillars in any human interaction. Therefore, it is important to be aware of the frequency and context in which reverse psychology is used, so as not to cross that line that can deteriorate the relationship or generate feelings of manipulation.

Furthermore, reverse psychology can be particularly sensitive when used on vulnerable people or in situations where there is an imbalance of power. For example, using this technique in a work environment, where a boss manipulates his employees into making decisions that favor the company without their knowledge, can be seen as an abuse of power. In these cases, the use of reverse psychology is not only unethical, but can have long-term negative consequences, such as loss of team morale or even legal problems if manipulative practices are discovered. In any situation where there is an imbalance of power, such as between parents and children, bosses and employees, or teachers and students, it is crucial that the use of reverse psychology is careful, respectful, and never used to exploit the other party.

Another important aspect is the emotional impact that reverse psychology can have on the person experiencing it. While in some situations it can be harmless, in others it can have negative emotional consequences. If a person feels that they have been manipulated into doing something they did not really want to do, they may feel deceived, which can lead to feelings of resentment or frustration. Furthermore, if reverse psychology is used too frequently in a relationship, the person may come to question whether their decisions are truly their own or whether they are always being influenced by others. This can negatively affect their self-esteem and their confidence in their own decision-making abilities. Therefore, it is essential to be aware of the emotional impact that using this technique can have and to ensure that it is not causing long-term psychological damage.

The use of reverse psychology should also be limited by cultural context. In some cultures or settings, manipulation, even if subtle, can be viewed as extremely negative. Every society has its own norms and values about honesty, manipulation, and respect for others. In some cultures, the idea of influencing another person's decisions without their knowledge can be viewed as disrespectful or even a form of deception. Therefore, before using reverse psychology in any situation, it is important to consider cultural norms and ensure that its use is not violating the values of the person or group you are interacting with. Being aware of these cultural differences is key to ensuring that reverse psychology is not perceived as manipulative or disrespectful.

Another important boundary is consent. Unlike other, more direct persuasion techniques, reverse psychology involves a degree of deception, as the person is not told directly what is expected of them. In situations where there is mutual trust or where decisions have significant consequences, it is critical that the person knows that their actions are being influenced in some way. Although it is not always possible to obtain "informed consent" when using reverse psychology, it is important that the other person has at least some idea that they are being guided in a certain direction. Respect for the other person's autonomy is essential, and the use of reverse psychology should not violate that principle.

Finally, it is important to remember that reverse psychology is not always the best solution. Sometimes, direct and honest communication is the best way to resolve a situation or influence another person's decisions. Trust and openness are fundamental values in relationships, whether personal or professional. While reverse psychology can be useful in certain situations, it should be seen as an additional tool, not the only strategy. In many cases, being transparent about what you want or expect from the other person can be more effective and ethical than trying to influence indirectly. The key is to find the right balance between persuasion and respect for the rights and autonomy of others.

In conclusion, the use of reverse psychology should be guided by sound ethical principles. Although it can be an effective technique in many situations, it is crucial to take into account the potential emotional effects, cultural context, and power implications. Furthermore, it is critical to remember that transparency and respect for the autonomy of others are essential to maintaining healthy, trust-based relationships. Using reverse psychology responsibly means being aware of its limits and ensuring that its use is not causing harm or manipulating people in negative ways. Like any tool, it should be used carefully, sensitively, and with deep respect for the people to whom it is applied.